thai

thai

a culinary journey of discovery

JUDY WILLIAMS

Love Food ™ is an imprint of Parragon Books Ltd

Parragon
Queen Street House
4 Queen Street
Bath BA1 1HE, UK

ISBN: 978-1-4054-9252-2
Printed in China

Produced by the Bridgewater Book Company Ltd

Photography: Clive Bozzard-Hill
Home economist: Valerie Barrett
Editorial advice: Pichit Rhatdanagkang and the Pailin Restaurant, Lewes

Notes for the Reader
This book uses imperial, metric, and US cup measurements. Follow the same units of measurement throughout; do not mix imperial and metric. All spoon measurements are level: teaspoons are assumed to be 5 ml, and tablespoons are assumed to be 15 ml. Unless otherwise stated, milk is assumed to be whole, eggs and individual vegetables such as potatoes are medium, and pepper is freshly ground black pepper. Recipes using raw or very lightly cooked eggs should be avoided by infants, the elderly, pregnant women, convalescents, and anyone suffering from an illness. The times given are an approximate guide only.

Picture Acknowledgments
The publisher would like to thank the following for permission to reproduce copyright material: William Manning/Corbis (pages 6–11, edges), Paul Anton/zefa/Corbis (page 13), Rusty Hill/PictureArts/Corbis (page 14), Andy Jones/zefa/Corbis (page 46), and Ian Garlick/StockFood Creative/Getty (page 84).

Take great care when preparing chiles, as the juice is very painful if transferred to eyes or other sensitive parts of the body. Wash your hands thoroughly after preparation. To avoid direct contact, use a fork to hold the chiles still while slicing and seeding with a sharp knife, or wear a new pair of rubber gloves.

Contents

Introduction

Thailand! Just the name sounds far away and exotic, and the reality certainly lives up to the country's impressive reputation, with its vast array of fabulous buildings, a fascinating history, beautiful countryside, and friendly people. In recent times, all the wealth that Thailand has to offer has come more easily within our reach, and many of us have been fortunate enough to visit the country, see the sights, and sample the fantastic food. Thai food is an Asian cuisine vibrant with sharp, fresh flavors. Full of variety, it can be chile hot, astringent with lime leaves, or creamy with coconut,

There are several different regions in Thailand, which offer a variety of types of food and methods of cooking according to the climate, the crops grown, and the natural resources that are available. Northern Thailand is where most of the country's wheat is grown, and less coconut milk is available, resulting in curries that are relatively thin in consistency. By contrast, the palm trees of the rainforests in the south produce a plentiful supply of coconut milk, which is put to good use in the local diet. The central, flatter region is where most of the rice eaten in Thailand is grown, as well as a mix of fruit and vegetables. Traditionally, the inhabitants of the poorer parts of the country, and in particular the northeast, used snails, grasshoppers, ants' eggs, and other wildlife in their cooking.

Luckily, we don't have to travel to Thailand to enjoy the taste of homemade Thai cooking. Specialist food stores offer Thai spices, seasonings, sauces, rice, and many more ingredients, and larger supermarkets also stock some of these goods.

Equipment

Thai cooking doesn't require a range of specialist cooking equipment and mostly you will need only what you would use in your everyday cooking, which again makes it easy to cook your own Thai meals. But there are a few essential items that you will frequently use when cooking Thai food.

Most Thai dishes are cooked using a wok. These were traditionally made of steel and required seasoning and oiling to keep them in serviceable condition. However, there are many different types now available, including good-quality nonstick varieties, which you will find in kitchen stores and supermarkets. Choose a large one so that there is plenty of room to toss the ingredients about when stir-frying, as well as enough capacity for the sauce. If you don't have a wok, you can use a large, preferably deep-sided, skillet instead.

A food processor is very useful for making curry pastes and fish cakes, as the texture needs to be as smooth as possible. If you have a small blender, this is especially useful for preparing curry pastes because it has a smaller base than a food processor, which prevents the ingredients being whizzed around everywhere.

While you can use ordinary kitchen knives for preparing ingredients, an Asian-style cleaver is a highly efficient tool for cutting vegetables into thin sticks, in addition to cutting meat into thin slices or cubes, and skinning fish. Otherwise, make sure that your standard knives are well sharpened.

You will need a large amount of cutting-board capacity for preparing the multiple ingredients used in many Thai dishes. It is a good idea, therefore, to keep a range of cutting boards and to color-code them for efficiency and hygiene.

Key ingredients

Coconut

Coconut milk and creamed coconut are used to enrich Thai dishes instead of milk, cream, or cheese. Creamed coconut comes in a solid block and needs dissolving in boiling water before using, or it can be added to simmering liquid. Coconut milk is available in cans, but it often separates in the can, so shake well before use. Stock is also widely used, often in combination with coconut milk, and in some recipes ingredients are added directly to the stock and/or coconut milk without any initial cooking in oil. This can render meat or poultry very tender and succulent, such as the chicken in Green chicken curry on page 38. Stocks can be homemade, purchased ready made from supermarkets, or created by dissolving stock cubes or stock powder in boiling water.

Oil

Use peanut or vegetable oil for stir-frying, pan-frying, and deep-frying, as it heats up to a high temperature safely. Olive oil will burn before it is sufficiently hot enough. Sesame oil is usually added to marinades or during cooking since, again, it does not withstand heat well. It also has a very pronounced flavor that could easily overwhelm the subtle taste of some of the dishes.

Noodles and rice

All main Thai dishes are served with noodles or rice, and it is entirely up to you which you choose for an accompaniment, although some recipes are better suited to one or the other. Egg noodles come in different thicknesses and this affects their cooking time to a slight degree, but they are all cooked in lightly salted boiling water and simmered for just a few minutes. They do have a tendency to stick together once drained, so it is often worth tossing them in a little sesame oil

or soy sauce to lubricate them. Once the noodles are served with the main dish, the sauce will also help to separate them. Rice noodles are more transparent and again come in various thicknesses. They are usually prepared by soaking in a pan of boiling water, covered, for a few minutes before draining and adding to a dish.

Jasmine rice, often called Thai fragrant rice, and basmati rice are the most frequently used rice varieties in Thai cooking. These are both long-grain rices that are aromatic and flavorsome. Jasmine rice is slightly sticky and fluffy once cooked, while basmati rice remains firm and separate. Cooking guidelines are given in the individual recipes, but always check the package directions, as cooking times can vary. To test whether rice is cooked, pinch a grain and bite it to see if it is tender, or when squeezed between the fingers it should break into three pieces.

Basic flavorings

Chiles

These come in different shapes and sizes, but generally the smaller they are, the hotter they will be. Start with the widely available larger, long pointed red and green chiles, as these are the mildest. Scotch bonnet chiles are the deceptive ones, as they are large, very colorful, and shapely but also blazingly hot. If you don't like your food too hot, feel free to reduce the amount of chile in a recipe. The same applies to garlic, but don't remove it altogether, as this will affect the end result.

Thai fish sauce

This widely used flavoring is made from small fish and shrimp that have been fermented in the sun. It is very salty and has a strong flavor, so use it in moderation.

Jaggery or palm sugar

This is produced from palm flowers and is not as sweet as cane sugars. If you cannot find jaggery, use dark brown sugar.

Cilantro

Fresh cilantro, with its bright green color and fresh, fragrant flavor, is the key herb used in Thai cooking. Use the stems as well as the leaves. Look out for cilantro with the roots attached, sold in Asian food stores, which offers the full flavor of the herb and is ideal for using in curry pastes.

Thai basil

Also known as holy basil, Thai basil is a wonderfully fragrant herb with a mild anise flavor, which adds an extra dimension to dishes. Use ordinary basil when Thai basil is unavailable.

Kaffir lime leaves

These glossy, dark green leaves have a citrus flavor, which gives a distinctive depth to Thai dishes. Fresh leaves have a much more pronounced, superior flavor to the dried variety.

Lemongrass

This is another classic Thai herb, with a pungent lemony flavor. The outer leaves of the stalks can be dry and tough, so remove them and use the inner soft parts if you are chopping it up. The stalks can also be bruised to help release their flavor before adding to dishes, but remove the stalks before serving.

Won ton and egg roll skins

Wrappers for won tons and the larger variety for egg rolls have become more widely available in recent times. Both freeze well. When working with them, keep the ones not in current use covered with plastic wrap, as they dry out quickly.

Curry pastes

Most Thai recipes use some sort of curry paste, and there are several types you can use. As well as the green and red pastes used in this book, there is yellow curry paste, Masaman curry paste (a well-known blend of flavors), and Panang. These are all smooth, very thick pastes that are strongly flavored, so you need to use only a small amount in a dish. Thai curry pastes are available from most large supermarkets, but small Asian food stores or Internet suppliers stock the authentic products, or you can make your own.

Green curry paste

1 tbsp coriander seeds
1 tbsp cumin seeds
12 fresh green Thai chiles, chopped
5 garlic cloves, chopped
2 lemongrass stalks, chopped
5 fresh kaffir lime leaves, chopped
handful of fresh cilantro, chopped
finely grated rind of 1 lime
1 tsp salt
1 tsp black peppercorns, crushed

Heat a dry skillet until hot. Add the coriander and cumin seeds, then cook over medium–high heat, shaking the skillet frequently, for 2–3 minutes, or until starting to pop. Put the toasted seeds with all the remaining ingredients in a food processor or small blender and process to a thick, smooth paste. Transfer to a screw-top glass jar and store in the refrigerator for up to a week.

Red curry paste

1 tbsp coriander seeds
1 tbsp cumin seeds
12 dried red chiles, chopped
2 shallots, chopped
6 garlic cloves, chopped
1-inch/2.5-cm piece fresh gingerroot, peeled and chopped
2 lemongrass stalks, chopped
4 fresh kaffir lime leaves, chopped
handful of fresh cilantro, chopped
finely grated rind of 1 lime
1 tsp salt
1 tsp black peppercorns, crushed

Heat a dry skillet until hot. Add the coriander and cumin seeds, then cook over medium–high heat, shaking the skillet frequently, for 2–3 minutes, or until starting to pop. Put the toasted seeds with all the remaining ingredients in a food processor or small blender and process to a thick, smooth paste. Transfer to a screw-top glass jar and store in the refrigerator for up to a week.

Appetizers

Appetizers should be tasty and small—just enough to whet the appetite before the main meal, and Thai cooking offers lots of ideal options. Many come perfectly packaged in pockets or wrappings of crisp pastry or omelet, others handily sized in the form of little cakes or on skewers, and most are served with a flavorful sauce for dipping.

If you are entertaining on a relatively large scale, you can make a selection of these finger foods, rather like canapés, so that everyone can try a variety of different dishes. But if serving two or four people, a single recipe is easier to prepare and it will still satisfy your guests.

Spicy Thai pockets

Kai yad sai talay

Serves 4

Omelets

4 eggs

2 tbsp water

3 scallions, finely chopped

small handful of fresh cilantro, finely chopped

peanut or vegetable oil, for pan-frying

soy sauce, to serve

Filling

3 scallions, coarsely chopped

8 oz/225 g raw squid, cleaned and cut into chunks if large or rings if small

4 oz/115 g raw shrimp, shelled and deveined

4 oz/115 g skinned white fish fillet, such as cod or coley, cut into 1-inch/2.5-cm cubes

1 head bok choy, coarsely chopped

1 tbsp green curry paste

1 tsp Thai fish sauce

You will need a good-quality nonstick 8-inch/20-cm skillet to make these omelets successfully, because they need to slide out easily onto a plate or cutting board.

Preheat the oven to 375°F/190°C. For the omelets, beat the eggs, water, scallions, and half the cilantro together in a bowl. Heat 1 tablespoon of oil in an 8-inch/20-cm nonstick skillet. Drizzle a quarter of the egg mixture over the bottom of the skillet to make a rough lacy pattern. Cook over medium–high heat for 2 minutes, or until just set, then use a spatula to turn the omelet over and cook on the other side for 1 minute. Slide out onto a plate or cutting board. Repeat with the remaining mixture to make 3 more omelets and add to the plate or board.

For the filling, heat 1 tablespoon of oil in the skillet. Add the scallions and all the seafood, then cook over medium heat, stirring frequently, for 2–3 minutes, or until the squid is firm, the shrimp have turned pink, and the fish is just cooked through. Transfer to a food processor and process for 30 seconds, or until just mixed. Add the bok choy, the remaining cilantro, the curry paste, and fish sauce and process again to a coarse mixture.

Arrange the omelets on a cutting board and put a quarter of the seafood mixture in the center of each. Roll one side of each omelet over the filling and fold in the adjacent "sides" to cover the filling, then fold up the omelet to make a small, square pocket. Transfer the pockets to a cookie sheet.

Bake in the preheated oven for 10–15 minutes, or until lightly browned and cooked through. Serve immediately with soy sauce.

Hot and sour soup

Tom yum

Serves 4

2 fresh red chiles, seeded and coarsely chopped

6 tbsp rice vinegar

5 cups vegetable stock

2 lemongrass stalks, halved

4 tbsp soy sauce

1 tbsp jaggery

juice of 1/2 lime

2 tbsp peanut or vegetable oil

8 oz/225 g firm tofu (drained weight), cut into 1/2-inch/1-cm cubes

14 oz/400 g canned straw mushrooms, drained

4 scallions, chopped

1 small head bok choy, shredded

This is a traditional, very popular Thai soup, with the heat provided by the chiles and sourness by the vinegar. Vary the balance of flavors according to your taste.

Mix the chiles and vinegar together in a nonreactive bowl. Cover and let stand at room temperature for 1 hour.

Meanwhile, bring the stock to a boil in a pan. Add the lemongrass, soy sauce, sugar, and lime juice, then reduce the heat and simmer for 20–30 minutes.

Heat the oil in a preheated wok, then add the tofu cubes and stir-fry over high heat for 2–3 minutes, or until browned all over. (You may need to do this in 2 batches, depending on the size of the wok.) Remove with a slotted spoon and drain on paper towels.

Add the chiles and vinegar with the tofu, mushrooms, and half the scallions to the stock mixture and cook for 10 minutes. Mix the remaining scallions with the bok choy and sprinkle over the soup before serving.

Cook's tip
If you can't find canned straw mushrooms, use whole baby white mushrooms or quartered standard-sized white mushrooms instead.

Crab, pork, and chile fritters

Tod man moo sai boo

Serves 4

4 oz/115 g canned white
crabmeat, drained

1/2 cup fresh ground pork

2 fresh red chiles, seeded
and coarsely chopped

1 tsp salt

2 scallions, chopped

handful of fresh cilantro, chopped

1 egg white

peanut or vegetable oil,
for pan-frying

Dipping sauce

2/3 cup water

4 tbsp superfine sugar

1 tbsp rice vinegar

1/2 small red onion,
very finely diced

2-inch/5-cm piece cucumber,
very finely diced

These delicious fritters can be made the day before and chilled in the refrigerator overnight to let the flavors develop. Cook and serve on the day of eating.

Put all the fritter ingredients except the oil in a food processor and process to a coarse paste. Use damp hands to shape into 20 small, flat cakes.

Heat enough oil to cover the bottom of a large skillet. Add the fritters, in 2–3 batches, and cook over medium–high heat for 2 minutes on each side, or until browned and cooked through. Remove with a slotted spoon and drain on paper towels, then keep warm while you cook the remaining fritters.

Meanwhile, to make the dipping sauce, put the water, sugar, and vinegar in a small pan and heat gently until the sugar has dissolved. Add the onion and cucumber and simmer for 5 minutes. Serve warm or cold in a small serving dish with the fritters.

Cook's tip

If you are making a large quantity of these fritters for a dinner party, cook them in several batches and transfer to a roasting pan. Warm them all up together in a hot oven until thoroughly heated through, and serve immediately.

Stir-fried shrimp with garlic

Gung ga tiem

Serves 2

2 tbsp peanut or vegetable oil

2 garlic cloves, finely chopped

1/2 onion, finely chopped

2 scallions, roughly chopped

pinch of salt

8 oz/225 g raw jumbo shrimp, shelled and deveined

3 tbsp soy sauce

1 tbsp jaggery

1 tsp Thai fish sauce

handful of fresh cilantro, chopped

The successful marrying of the flavors of shrimp and garlic ensures that this is a popular appetizer. The dish can be made with ordinary large shrimp, but use jumbo shrimp if possible, as they are more succulent.

Heat the oil in a preheated wok. Add the garlic, onion, and scallions, then stir-fry over medium–high heat for 30 seconds. Add the remaining ingredients and half the cilantro and stir-fry over high heat for 2–3 minutes, or until the shrimp have turned pink.

Remove from the heat, then stir in the remaining cilantro and serve immediately.

Cook's tip

Serve onto hot plates, as this will help keep the dish hotter for longer. Cook the shrimp quickly, as they toughen if cooked for too long.

Vegetable and black bean egg rolls

Por pia pak

Serves 4

2 tbsp peanut or vegetable oil, plus extra for deep-frying

4 scallions, cut into 2-inch/ 5-cm lengths and shredded lengthwise, plus extra to garnish

1-inch/2.5-cm piece fresh gingerroot, peeled and finely chopped

1 large carrot, peeled and cut into thin sticks

1 red bell pepper, seeded and cut into thin sticks

6 tbsp black bean sauce

1/3 cup fresh bean sprouts

7 oz/200 g canned water chestnuts, drained and coarsely chopped

2-inch/5-cm piece cucumber, cut into thin sticks

8 x 8-inch/20-cm square egg roll skins

sweet chili dipping sauce, to serve (optional)

Egg rolls can be made with all sorts of fillings, so it's easy to adapt the ingredients as long as you keep the mixture fairly dry. Too much sauce and the pastry will become soggy.

Heat the oil in a preheated wok. Add the scallions, ginger, carrot, and red bell pepper, then stir-fry over medium–high heat for 2–3 minutes. Add the black bean sauce, bean sprouts, water chestnuts, and cucumber and stir-fry for 1–2 minutes. Let cool.

Remove the egg roll skins from the package, but keep them in a pile and covered with plastic wrap to prevent them drying out. Lay one skin on a counter in front of you in a diamond shape and brush the edges with water. Put a spoonful of the filling near one corner and fold the corner over the filling. Roll over again and then fold the side corners over the filling. Roll up to seal the filling completely. Repeat with the remaining skins and filling.

Heat the oil for deep-frying in the wok or a deep pan or deep-fat fryer to 350–375°F/ 180–190°C, or until a cube of bread browns in 30 seconds. Add the rolls, in 2–3 batches, and cook for 2–3 minutes, or until crisp and golden all over. Remove with a slotted spoon and drain on paper towels, then keep warm while you cook the remaining rolls. Garnish with shredded scallions and serve with sweet chili dipping sauce, if using.

Crispy pork dumplings

Kanom jeeb moo grob

Serves 4

5 small fresh red chiles

3 scallions, coarsely chopped

1 garlic clove, coarsely chopped

generous 1 cup fresh ground pork

1 tsp salt

20 won ton skins

peanut or vegetable oil,
for deep-frying

These dumplings can be steamed and then broiled if you prefer, but they are quicker to cook and crisper to eat when deep-fried.

To make the chile flowers for the garnish, use a sharp knife to make 6–8 slits about 1/2 inch/ 1 cm in length from the stem end to the tip of four of the chiles. Put them into a bowl of iced water and soak for 30 minutes until they have expanded into flower shapes.

To make the dumplings, seed and coarsely chop the remaining chile, then put it into a food processor with the scallions, garlic, pork, and salt and process to a smooth paste.

Remove the won ton skins from the package, but keep them in a pile and covered with plastic wrap to prevent them drying out. Lay one skin on a counter in front of you in a diamond shape and brush the edges with water. Put a small amount of filling near one edge and fold the skin over the filling. Press the edges together to seal the pocket and shape into a semicircle. Repeat with the remaining skins and filling.

Heat the oil in a wok or a deep pan or deep-fat fryer to 350–375°F/180–190°C, or until a cube of bread browns in 30 seconds. Add the dumplings, in batches, and cook for 45 seconds–1 minute, or until crisp and golden all over. Remove with a slotted spoon and drain on paper towels, then keep warm while you cook the remaining dumplings. Serve immediately once they are all cooked, garnished with the chile flowers.

Cook's tip

Always check the temperature of the oil before deep-frying. If the oil is smoking, it is too hot. Remove from the heat and let cool a little. Do not add too many dumplings at a time, otherwise the temperature of the oil will drop and this will make the dumplings soggy.

Chicken satay skewers with peanut sauce

Satay gai

Serves 4

4 skinless, boneless chicken breasts, about 4 oz/115 g each, cut into ¾-inch/2-cm cubes

4 tbsp soy sauce

1 tbsp cornstarch

2 garlic cloves, finely chopped

1-inch/2.5-cm piece fresh gingerroot, peeled and finely chopped

cucumber, coarsely chopped, to serve

Peanut sauce

2 tbsp peanut or vegetable oil

½ onion, finely chopped

1 garlic clove, finely chopped

4 tbsp crunchy peanut butter

4–5 tbsp water

½ tsp chili powder

This is a simplified version of the ever-popular appetizer served in Thai restaurants. Marinating the chicken adds extra flavor.

Put the chicken cubes in a shallow dish. Mix the soy sauce, cornstarch, garlic, and ginger together in a small bowl and pour over the chicken. Cover and let marinate in the refrigerator for at least 2 hours. Meanwhile, soak 12 bamboo skewers in cold water for at least 30 minutes.

Preheat the oven to 375°F/190°C. Divide the chicken cubes between the bamboo skewers. Heat a ridged grill pan until hot, then add the skewers and cook over high heat for 3–4 minutes, turning occasionally, until browned all over. Transfer the skewers to a cookie sheet and cook in the preheated oven for 5–8 minutes, or until cooked through.

Meanwhile, to make the sauce, heat the oil in a pan, then add the onion and garlic and cook over medium heat, stirring frequently, for 3–4 minutes, or until softened. Add the peanut butter, water, and chili powder and simmer for 2–3 minutes, or until softened and thinned.

Serve the skewers immediately with the warm sauce and the cucumber.

Cook's tip
Presoaking the bamboo skewers will help prevent them burning. You can also cut any excess length from the skewers if they are too long so that they fit within the grill pan; this will stop the exposed ends burning.

Shrimp wraps

Gung gra borg

Serves 4

24 cooked tail-on (shelled and
tails left intact) jumbo shrimp

2 tbsp sweet chili dipping sauce

24 won ton skins

peanut or vegetable oil,
for deep-frying

Dipping sauce

1 tbsp sesame oil

3 tbsp soy sauce

1/2-inch/1-cm piece fresh
gingerroot, peeled and finely
chopped

1 scallion, finely chopped

Crisp pastry wrapped around succulent shrimp makes a winning combination,
and the dip adds heat and sweetness.

Toss the shrimp in the chili sauce in a bowl.
Remove the skins from the package, but keep
them in a pile and covered with plastic wrap
to prevent them drying out. Lay one skin on
a counter in front of you and brush the edges
with water. Place a shrimp diagonally across the
square and fold the skin around the shrimp to
enclose it completely, leaving the tail extended.
Repeat with the remaining skins and shrimp.

Heat the oil in a wok or a deep pan or
deep-fat fryer to 350–375°F/180–190°C,
or until a cube of bread browns in 30 seconds.
Add the wraps, in batches, and cook for
45 seconds–1 minute, or until crisp and golden
all over. Remove with a slotted spoon and drain
on paper towels, then keep warm while you
cook the remaining wraps.

Meanwhile, to make the dipping sauce, mix
the sesame oil, soy sauce, ginger, and scallion
together in a bowl. Serve in small serving bowls
with the wraps.

Roasted sticky chicken wings

Peek gai ob

Serves 4

12 chicken wings

3 tbsp tomato paste

3 tbsp soy sauce

1 tbsp jaggery

2 tbsp sweet chili dipping sauce

generous 1 cup jasmine rice

2 tbsp rice vinegar

few fresh Thai basil leaves, chopped, plus extra whole leaves to garnish

peanut or vegetable oil, for pan-frying

It is always a particularly gratifying experience eating food with your fingers, and these sticky, sweet wings are a real treat. Make sure that you have plenty of napkins and a finger bowl for guests.

Trim off the pointed tips of the wings, then arrange the wings in a roasting pan.

Mix the tomato paste, soy sauce, sugar, and chili sauce together in a small bowl and spoon over the chicken. Cover and let marinate in the refrigerator for 3 hours or overnight.

Meanwhile, cook the rice in a large pan of lightly salted boiling water for 12–15 minutes until tender, or according to the package directions. Drain, then return to the pan and stir in the vinegar and chopped basil.

Line a baking pan or shallow dish about 7½ inches/19 cm square with plastic wrap. Press the rice into the pan or dish in an even layer about 1 inch/2.5 cm deep. Cover and let chill in the refrigerator while the chicken wings are marinating. Turn out of the pan and cut into 1-inch/2.5-cm cubes, then set aside.

Preheat the oven to 400°F/200°C. Roast the chicken wings in the preheated oven for 30–35 minutes, or until slightly blackened and sticky, tender, and the juices run clear when a skewer is inserted into the thickest part of the meat.

Meanwhile, heat a little oil in a small pan or skillet. Add the whole basil leaves and cook over medium–high heat, stirring, for a few seconds until crispy. Serve the chicken wings hot with the rice cubes, topped with the crispy basil leaves.

Crab won tons

Kaiw phoo

Serves 4

1 tbsp peanut or vegetable oil, plus extra for deep-frying

1-inch/2.5-cm piece fresh gingerroot, peeled and finely chopped

1/4 red bell pepper, seeded and finely chopped

handful of fresh cilantro, chopped

1/4 tsp salt

5 1/2 oz/150 g canned white crabmeat, drained

20 won ton skins

soy sauce or sweet chili dipping sauce, to serve

The sweetness of the crabmeat combined with the crunch of the red bell pepper make these little pockets a tasty surprise to bite into.

Heat the oil in a preheated wok, then add the ginger and red bell pepper and stir-fry over high heat for 30 seconds. Add the cilantro and mix well. Let cool, then add the salt and crabmeat and mix well.

Remove the skins from the package, but keep them in a pile and covered with plastic wrap to prevent them drying out. Lay one skin on a counter in front of you and brush the edges with water. Put a teaspoonful of the crabmeat mixture in the center and fold the skin over the mixture to form a triangle. Press the edges together to seal. Fold each side corner up to the top corner to make a small pocket, brushing the edges with water to seal if necessary. Repeat with the remaining skins and crabmeat mixture.

Heat the oil for deep-frying in the wok or a deep pan or deep-fat fryer to 350–375°F/ 180–190°C, or until a cube of bread browns in 30 seconds. Add the won tons, in batches, and cook for 45 seconds–1 minute, or until crisp and golden all over. Remove with a slotted spoon and drain on paper towels, then keep warm while you cook the remaining won tons. Serve with soy sauce or sweet chili dipping sauce.

Cook's tip
If fresh crabmeat is available, use instead of the canned crabmeat, but the latter is fine to use otherwise.

Main Meals

Curries are obviously firm favorites when it comes to Thai main courses and the recipes featured include a classic Green chicken curry, together with that other great traditional dish, Masaman curry (with tender beef, peanut, and potatoes), as well as a sumptuous Mixed fish and coconut curry. But there are other types of equally flavorful dishes, such as aromatic stir-fries and the irresistible Crispy roast duck—in this case served with wickedly fiery yet sweet pickled plums.

When cooking for a crowd, feel free to combine one of these recipes with a dish from the Rice and Noodles section, or serve with some of those invitingly crisp pockets from the Appetizers chapter.

Angler fish kabobs with red bell peppers and shrimp

Mai talay

The dense texture of angler fish makes it excellent for threading onto kabobs, and it also absorbs flavors very effectively when marinated.

Serves 4

2 red bell peppers, seeded and cut lengthwise into 6 wedges

12 oz/350 g angler fish tail

juice of 1/2 lime

1 tsp red curry paste

handful of fresh cilantro, chopped, plus a few sprigs to garnish

8 oz/225 g raw shell-on jumbo shrimp

To serve

cooked rice

stir-fried vegetables (optional)

Soak 12 bamboo skewers in cold water for at least 30 minutes. Meanwhile, arrange the red bell pepper wedges, skin-side up, on a cookie sheet and cook under a preheated hot broiler for 5–8 minutes, or until the skin is blackened. Let cool, then peel off the skin. Cut the flesh into 1-inch/2.5-cm squares.

Peel the gray membrane off the angler fish and discard. Cut down either side of the central bone to make 2 long pieces of fish. Cut into 1-inch/2.5-cm cubes.

Mix the lime juice, curry paste, and cilantro together in a large bowl. Add the fish cubes and toss to coat in the mixture. Thread the red bell pepper wedges, angler fish, and shrimp alternately onto the bamboo skewers. Cover and let marinate in the refrigerator for 30 minutes.

Cook the kabobs in a preheated ridged grill pan over medium–high heat or under a preheated medium–high broiler, turning occasionally, for 4–5 minutes, or until browned all over and cooked through. Garnish with cilantro sprigs and serve immediately on a bed of rice with stir-fried vegetables, if using.

Green chicken curry

Gang kaiw wan gai

Serves 4

2 tbsp peanut or vegetable oil

4 scallions, coarsely chopped

2 tbsp green curry paste

3 cups canned coconut milk

1 chicken stock cube

6 skinless, boneless chicken breasts, about 4 oz/115 g each, cut into 1-inch/2.5-cm cubes

large handful of fresh cilantro, chopped

1 tsp salt

cooked rice or noodles, to serve

A very popular Thai dish that is easy to prepare and tastes fantastic. Poaching the chicken makes it very tender and the lime leaves add a tangy twist to the sauce.

Heat the oil in a preheated wok. Add the scallions and stir-fry over medium–high heat for 30 seconds, or until starting to soften.

Add the curry paste, coconut milk, and stock cube and bring gently to a boil, stirring occasionally. Add the chicken cubes, half the cilantro, and the salt and stir well. Reduce the heat and simmer gently for 8–10 minutes, or until the chicken is cooked through and tender. Stir in the remaining cilantro. Serve immediately with rice or noodles.

Cook's tip

Use red curry paste if you like a hotter flavor. Other vegetables can be added and cooked in the coconut milk sauce.

Spicy beef with black bean sauce

Nue pud tao jaiw

Serves 2

2 tbsp peanut or vegetable oil

2 onions, cut into wedges

2 garlic cloves, finely chopped

1 tsp pepper

1 lb/450 g beef tenderloin, cut into thick strips

2 oz/55 g baby corn, halved lengthwise

4 oz/115 g shiitake mushrooms, thickly sliced

6 tbsp soy sauce

1/2 cup black bean sauce

1 tsp jaggery

chopped fresh cilantro, to garnish

cooked medium egg noodles, to serve

The delicious taste of black bean sauce is wonderful with tender beef and shiitake mushrooms. Baby corn add extra flavor, texture, and color.

Heat the oil in a preheated wok. Add the onions and stir-fry over medium–high heat for 2–3 minutes, or until starting to soften.

Add the garlic and pepper and stir well, then add the beef strips, baby corn, and mushrooms and stir-fry over high heat for 2–3 minutes. Add half the soy sauce, the black bean sauce, and sugar and stir-fry for 1–2 minutes.

Serve immediately with egg noodles tossed in the remaining soy sauce, and garnished with chopped cilantro.

Cook's tip
This dish is equally tasty served with egg-fried rice or cilantro rice.

Chili shrimp with garlic noodles

Guay taiw phud gung

Serves 4

7 oz/200 g cooked, shelled, and
deveined jumbo shrimp

4 tbsp sweet chili dipping sauce

4 tbsp peanut or vegetable oil

4 scallions, chopped

2 oz/55 g snow peas, trimmed and
halved diagonally

1 tbsp red curry paste

1¾ cups canned
coconut milk

2 oz/55 g canned, drained
bamboo shoots

⅓ cup fresh bean sprouts

Garlic noodles

4 oz/115 g dried medium
egg noodles

2 garlic cloves, crushed

handful of fresh cilantro, chopped

A hot and spicy dish for those chile enthusiasts! The crunchy snow peas and bean sprouts complement the hot flavors well.

Toss the shrimp with the chili sauce in a bowl. Cover and set aside.

Heat half the oil in a preheated wok. Add the scallions and snow peas, then stir-fry over medium–high heat for 2–3 minutes. Add the curry paste and stir well. Pour in the coconut milk and bring gently to a boil, stirring occasionally. Add the bamboo shoots and bean sprouts and cook, stirring, for 1 minute. Stir in the shrimp and chili sauce, then reduce the heat and simmer for 1–2 minutes, or until just heated through.

Meanwhile, for the noodles, cook in a pan of lightly salted boiling water for 4–5 minutes until just tender, or according to the package directions. Drain and return to the pan.

Heat the remaining oil in a small nonstick skillet, then add the garlic and stir-fry over high heat for 30 seconds. Add to the drained noodles with half the cilantro and toss together until well mixed.

Transfer the garlic noodles to 4 serving bowls. Top with the chili shrimp mixture, and serve immediately, garnished with the remaining cilantro.

Crispy roast duck and pickled plums

Ped grob gap plum dong

Serves 4

4 boneless duck breasts, about
6 oz/175 g each

3 scallions, finely chopped

2 garlic cloves, finely chopped

4 tbsp oyster sauce

1 tbsp peanut or vegetable oil

To serve

cooked noodles

stir-fried vegetables (optional)

Pickled plums

generous 1/4 cup superfine sugar

4 tbsp white wine vinegar

1 fresh red chile, seeded and
finely chopped

1/2 tsp salt

4 plums, pitted and cut into fourths

The pickled plums may sound complicated, but they are easy to prepare and make an ideal accompaniment to other dishes, such as cold meats. But be warned—the pickled plums are chile hot!

Use a sharp knife to make diagonal slashes in both directions in the skin of the duck breasts. Mix the scallions, garlic, and oyster sauce together in a small bowl and spread over the duck skin. Cover and let marinate in the refrigerator for 1 hour.

Meanwhile, to make the pickled plums, put all the ingredients except the plums in a pan and simmer gently for 10–15 minutes. Add the plums and simmer for an additional 5 minutes, or until just starting to soften. Let cool.

Preheat the oven to 400°F/200°C. Heat the oil in a large skillet, then add the duck breasts, skin-side down, and cook for 2–3 minutes, or until browned. Turn over and cook on the other side for 1–2 minutes.

Transfer the duck breasts to a roasting pan and roast in the preheated oven for 10–15 minutes, or until just cooked through. Remove from the oven, then cover with foil and let rest for 10 minutes.

Serve the duck breasts with the pickled plums, together with noodles and stir-fried vegetables, if using.

Gingered chicken with cashews and scallions

Gai phad met ma muang

This simple yet flavorful dish makes an ideal packed lunch, as it tastes as good cold as it does when served hot.

Serves 4

3-inch/7.5-cm piece fresh gingerroot, peeled and finely chopped

6 skinless, boneless chicken breasts, about 4 oz/115 g each, cut into 1-inch/2.5-cm cubes

2 tbsp sesame oil

4 tbsp peanut or vegetable oil

1 onion, thinly sliced

2 garlic cloves, crushed

4 oz/115 g mushrooms, sliced

1 tsp salt

1/4 head Chinese cabbage, roughly chopped

1 bunch of scallions, chopped

4 tbsp soy sauce

1 tsp Thai fish sauce

1 tsp jaggery

1/4 cup unsalted cashews

cooked rice or noodles, to serve (optional)

Mix the ginger, chicken cubes, and sesame oil together in a bowl. Cover and let marinate in the refrigerator for 2–3 hours.

Heat 3 tablespoons of the peanut or vegetable oil in a preheated wok. Add the onion and garlic and stir-fry over medium–high heat for 2–3 minutes. Add the chicken mixture and stir-fry over high heat for 2–3 minutes. Add the mushrooms, salt, Chinese cabbage, and half the scallions and stir-fry for 3–4 minutes. Add the soy sauce, fish sauce, and sugar and stir-fry for 2–3 minutes.

Meanwhile, heat the remaining peanut or vegetable oil in a separate preheated wok or skillet. Add the cashews and the remaining scallions and stir-fry over high heat for 1 minute, or until the cashews are golden and the scallions are crispy. Sprinkle over the chicken mixture before serving with rice or noodles, if using.

Ground pork kabobs with sweet chili dipping sauce

Moo kebab gab nam prik samrot

Serves 4

1 large onion, chopped

2 garlic cloves, crushed

2 cups fresh ground pork

1 tsp salt

2 tbsp sweet chili dipping sauce, plus extra to serve

handful of fresh cilantro, chopped, plus extra sprigs to garnish (optional)

1 egg

egg-fried rice, to serve

These tasty kabobs make a great centerpiece for a dinner party when arranged across each other on a bed of rice, garnished with fresh cilantro sprigs.

Put all the ingredients except the rice in a food processor and process to a thick paste.

Divide the pork mixture into 8 portions. Using damp hands, squeeze one portion evenly around a flat metal skewer to make 8 kabobs. Cover and chill in the refrigerator for at least 1 hour.

Cook the kabobs in a preheated ridged grill pan over medium–high heat or under a preheated medium–high broiler, turning occasionally, for 5–6 minutes, or until browned all over and cooked through. Serve immediately on a bed of egg-fried rice with sweet chili dipping sauce and, if desired, garnished with sprigs of fresh cilantro.

Cook's tip

Keep your hands damp with cold water to prevent the meat sticking to them as you form the pork mixture around the kabobs.

Mixed fish and coconut curry

Gang talay

Serves 4

2 tbsp peanut or vegetable oil

6 scallions, cut into 1-inch/
2.5-cm lengths

1 large carrot, peeled and cut
into thin sticks

2 oz/55 g green beans, trimmed
and cut into short lengths

2 tbsp red curry paste

3 cups canned coconut milk

8 oz/225 g skinned white fish fillet,
such as cod or coley, cut into
1-inch/2.5-cm cubes

8 oz/225 g squid, cleaned and cut
into thick rings

8 oz/225 g large raw shrimp,
shelled and deveined

1/3 cup fresh bean sprouts

4 oz/115 g dried rice noodles,
cooked according to the package
directions and drained

handful of fresh cilantro, chopped

handful of fresh Thai basil leaves,
to garnish

Coconut and fish complement each other well, and this recipe really brings out the flavor of both. The Thai basil adds a wonderful freshness to this curry.

Heat the oil in a preheated wok. Add the scallions, carrot, and green beans and stir-fry over medium–high heat for 2–3 minutes, or until starting to soften.

Stir in the curry paste, then add the coconut milk. Bring gently to a boil, stirring occasionally, then reduce the heat and simmer for

2–3 minutes. Add all the seafood and bean sprouts and simmer for 2–3 minutes, or until just cooked through and the shrimp have turned pink.

Stir in the cooked noodles and cilantro and cook for 1 minute. Serve immediately, sprinkled with the basil.

Masaman curry

Gang masaman

Serves 4

2 tbsp peanut or vegetable oil

8 oz/225 g shallots, coarsely chopped

1 garlic clove, crushed

1 lb/450 g beef tenderloin, thickly sliced and then cut into 1-inch/ 2.5-cm cubes

2 tbsp ready-made masaman curry paste

3 potatoes, peeled and cut into 1-inch/2.5-cm cubes

1³/₄ cups canned coconut milk

2 tbsp soy sauce

²/₃ cup beef stock

1 tsp jaggery

¹/₂ cup unsalted peanuts

handful of fresh cilantro, chopped

noodles or cooked rice, to serve

A very traditional dish that combines potatoes and peanuts with beef tenderloin, and tastes fantastic!

Heat the oil in a preheated wok. Add the shallots and garlic and stir-fry over medium–high heat for 1–2 minutes, or until softened. Add the beef cubes and curry paste and stir-fry over high heat for 2–3 minutes, or until browned all over. Add the potatoes, coconut milk, soy sauce, stock, and sugar and bring gently to a boil, stirring occasionally. Reduce the heat and simmer for 8–10 minutes, or until the potatoes are tender.

Meanwhile, heat a separate dry skillet until hot, then add the peanuts and cook over medium–high heat, shaking the skillet frequently, for 2–3 minutes, or until lightly browned. Add to the curry with the cilantro and stir well. Serve hot with noodles or cooked rice.

Cook's tip
To help the skins of the shallots come off more easily, put them in a heatproof bowl and cover with boiling water, then let stand for 10 minutes.

Roast pork with pineapple

Moo ob saparot

Serves 4

12 oz/350 g pork tenderloin

4 tbsp sweet chili dipping sauce

4 tbsp soy sauce

1 tsp sugar

2 tbsp peanut or vegetable oil

1 red onion, thinly sliced

1 carrot, peeled and cut into thin sticks

1 zucchini, cut into thin sticks

4 oz/115 g canned water chestnuts, drained and sliced

2 fresh pineapple rings, peeled, cored, and coarsely chopped

cooked rice, to serve

The chili flavour from the sauce and the sweetness from the pineapple make this a really fresh-tasting dish for summer evenings.

Put the pork in a shallow dish. Mix half the chili sauce, the soy sauce, and sugar together in a small bowl and brush over the pork. Cover and let marinate in the refrigerator overnight.

Preheat the oven to 400°F/200°C. Heat a ridged grill pan or skillet until hot, then add the pork and cook over high heat for 1 minute on each side, or until browned. Transfer to a roasting pan and roast in the preheated oven for 15–20 minutes, or until cooked through. Thinly slice the pork, then cut each slice into strips.

Heat the oil in a preheated wok, then add the onion, carrot, and zucchini and stir-fry over medium–high heat for 2–3 minutes. Add the water chestnuts, the remaining chili sauce, and the chopped pineapple rings and stir-fry for 1 minute. Add the pork and stir-fry for 1 minute. Serve immediately with rice.

Cook's tip
You can use canned pineapple, drained, instead of fresh in this dish.

Vegetarian

Thai food offers vegetarians a tasty, healthy, and flexible approach to cooking and is bursting with fragrant and fiery flavors as well as color and texture. Tofu, or soya bean curd, provides an excellent source of vegetable protein and can easily be infused with flavor by marinating. Unsalted cashews or peanuts are also highly nutritious and contribute an extra crunchiness to stir-fries and other Thai dishes.

Although the vegetables used can vary according to what is available and seasonal, some are used specifically for their particular qualities in the curry dishes, such as potato teamed with spinach.

Cauliflower, broccoli, and cashew salad

Yum dokralam metmamuang

This main dish is full of vitamins. Keep it crunchy by cooking the vegetables for a short length of time and adding the nuts at the last minute.

Serves 4

2 tbsp peanut or vegetable oil

2 red onions, cut into wedges

1 small head cauliflower, cut into florets

1 small head broccoli, cut into florets

2 tbsp ready-made yellow curry paste or red curry paste

1¾ cups canned coconut milk

1 tsp Thai fish sauce

1 tsp jaggery

1 tsp salt

½ cup unsalted cashews

handful of fresh cilantro, chopped, plus extra sprigs, torn, to garnish

Heat the oil in a preheated wok. Add the onions and stir-fry over medium–high heat for 3–4 minutes, or until starting to brown. Add the cauliflower and broccoli and stir-fry for 1–2 minutes. Stir in the curry paste and stir-fry for 30 seconds, then add the coconut milk, fish sauce, sugar, and salt. Bring gently to a boil, stirring occasionally, then reduce the heat and simmer gently for 3–4 minutes, or until the vegetables are almost tender.

Meanwhile, heat a separate dry skillet until hot. Add the cashews and cook, shaking the skillet frequently, for 2–3 minutes, or until lightly browned. Add to the stir-fry with the cilantro and stir well, then serve immediately, garnished with torn sprigs of cilantro.

Mixed mushrooms with spinach and bean sprouts

Pat puk ruamit

Serves 4

2 tbsp peanut or vegetable oil

1 bunch of scallions, coarsely chopped

1 garlic clove, crushed

1-inch/2.5-cm piece fresh gingerroot, peeled and finely chopped

6 oz/175 g shiitake mushrooms, halved

6 oz/175 g closed-cup mushrooms, quartered

6 oz/175 g baby white mushrooms

3 tbsp soy sauce

4 oz/115 g spinach leaves

1/3 cup fresh bean sprouts

2 tbsp sweet chili dipping sauce

noodles or cooked rice, to serve

Various different kinds of mushroom are now widely available, so try different combinations in this recipe for flavor and texture variation.

Heat the oil in a preheated wok. Add the scallions and stir-fry over medium–high heat for 1–2 minutes. Add the garlic and ginger and stir-fry for 1–2 minutes. Add all the mushrooms and stir-fry over high heat for 2–3 minutes, or until starting to soften and brown.

Add the soy sauce, spinach, and bean sprouts and stir-fry for 2–3 minutes, or until the spinach has wilted. Stir in the chili sauce. Serve immediately with noodles or rice.

Cook's tip

It is more economical to use spinach that you have to wash yourself, but if in a hurry, use the ready-washed variety.

Crispy vegetable stir-fry salad

Yum puk grob

Serves 4

2 tbsp peanut or vegetable oil

1 bunch of scallions,
coarsely chopped

1-inch/2.5-cm piece fresh
gingerroot, peeled and
finely chopped

2 lemongrass stalks, halved

2 carrots, peeled and cut into
thin sticks

1 small head broccoli,
cut into florets

2 oz/55 g baby corn,
halved lengthwise

2 oz/55 g canned water chestnuts,
drained

1 tbsp red curry paste

8 oz/225 g dried medium
egg noodles

4 tbsp sesame seeds

You can use any mix of vegetables for this stir-fry, according to what is available and looks appealing or what is on special offer on the day.

Heat the oil in a preheated wok. Add the scallions, ginger, and lemongrass and stir-fry over medium–high heat for 2–3 minutes, or until starting to soften. Add the carrots, broccoli, and baby corn and stir-fry for 3–4 minutes until starting to soften. Add the water chestnuts and curry paste and stir well, then stir-fry for an additional 2–3 minutes. Discard the lemongrass.

Meanwhile, cook the noodles in a large pan of lightly salted boiling water for 4–5 minutes until just tender, or according to the package directions. Drain and return to the pan. Add the sesame seeds and toss to coat.

Add the noodles to the stir-fried vegetables and serve immediately.

Cook's tip
Cut all the vegetables to a similiar size so that they cook in the same length of time.

Chunky potato and spinach curry

Gang puk

Serves 4

4 tomatoes

2 tbsp peanut or vegetable oil

2 onions, cut into thick wedges

1-inch/2.5-cm piece fresh gingerroot, peeled and finely chopped

1 garlic clove, chopped

2 tbsp ground coriander

1 lb/450 g peeled potatoes, cut into chunks

2¹/₂ cups vegetable stock

1 tbsp red curry paste

8 oz/225 g spinach leaves

cooked rice or noodles, to serve (optional)

Potatoes in curry are always delicious, but become sublime when mixed with spinach. A favorite combination in Indian curries, it works equally well in Thai cooking.

Put the tomatoes in a heatproof bowl and cover with boiling water. Leave for 2–3 minutes, then plunge into cold water and peel off the skins. Cut each tomato into quarters and remove and discard the seeds and central core. Set aside.

Heat the oil in a preheated wok. Add the onions, ginger, and garlic and stir-fry over medium–high heat for 2–3 minutes, or until starting to soften. Add the coriander and potatoes and stir-fry for 2–3 minutes. Add the stock and curry paste and bring to a boil, stirring occasionally. Reduce the heat and simmer gently for 10–15 minutes, or until the potatoes are tender.

Add the spinach and the tomato quarters and cook, stirring, for 1 minute, or until the spinach has wilted. Serve with rice or noodles, if using.

Peanut tofu skewers

Tofu tua barbecue

Serves 4

8 oz/225 g firm tofu
(drained weight), cut into
1-inch/2.5-cm cubes

1 tbsp peanut or vegetable oil

5 tbsp soy sauce

1 fresh red chile, seeded
and sliced

1 garlic clove, crushed

2 tbsp crunchy peanut butter

2 red bell peppers, seeded and cut
into 1-inch/2.5-cm squares

1 zucchini, cut into thick slices

6 oz/175 g dried rice noodles

3 tbsp sweet chili dipping sauce

1/2 cucumber, chopped

1/3 cup unsalted peanuts, chopped

handful of fresh cilantro, chopped,
to garnish

Tofu absorbs marinades well, which gives it more flavor, since otherwise it can be rather bland. It is also firm enough to remain on the skewers if cooked quickly.

Pat the tofu cubes dry with paper towels. Put the oil, soy sauce, chile, garlic, and peanut butter in a food processor and process to a paste. Transfer to a bowl and stir the tofu cubes into the marinade. Cover and let marinate in the refrigerator for 1 hour. Meanwhile, soak 8 bamboo skewers in cold water.

Thread the tofu cubes, red bell pepper squares, and zucchini slices alternately onto the skewers and brush with any remaining marinade. Cook in a preheated ridged grill pan over medium–high heat or under a preheated medium–high broiler, turning occasionally, for 3–4 minutes, or until browned all over.

Meanwhile, soak the noodles in a pan of boiling water, covered, for 4 minutes, or according to the package directions.

Drain the noodles and transfer to a bowl. Add the chili sauce, cucumber, and peanuts and toss to coat. Divide between 4 serving plates and top with 2 skewers each. Serve immediately, garnished with the cilantro.

Butternut squash curry

Gang butternut

Serves 4

2 tbsp peanut or vegetable oil

1 tsp cumin seeds

2 red onions, sliced

2 celery stalks, sliced

1 large butternut squash, peeled, seeded, and cut into chunks

2 tbsp green curry paste

1¼ cups vegetable stock

2 fresh kaffir lime leaves

⅓ cup fresh bean sprouts

handful of fresh cilantro, chopped, to garnish

cooked rice, to serve

The bright orange of the squash and the green of the celery make this a colorful dish to serve. The lime leaves add an intense citrus flavor.

Heat the oil in a preheated wok, then add the cumin seeds and stir-fry over medium–high heat for 2–3 minutes, or until starting to pop. Add the onions and celery and stir-fry for 2–3 minutes. Add the squash and stir-fry for 3–4 minutes. Add the curry paste, stock, and lime leaves and bring to a boil, stirring occasionally.

Reduce the heat and simmer gently for 3–4 minutes, or until the squash is tender. Add the bean sprouts and cook for an additional 1–2 minutes, or until hot but still crunchy. Sprinkle the cilantro over the curry and serve with rice.

Cook's tip

It is easier to peel the squash if you cut it into pieces first, as it is very hard. Use a small, sharp knife rather than a vegetable peeler.

Eggplant curry

Gang makua

Serves 2

peanut or vegetable oil, for deep-frying, plus 2 tbsp

2 eggplants, cut into ³/₄-inch/2-cm cubes

1 bunch of scallions, coarsely chopped

2 garlic cloves, chopped

2 red bell peppers, seeded and cut into ³/₄-inch/2-cm squares

3 zucchini, thickly sliced

1³/₄ cups canned coconut milk

2 tbsp red curry paste

large handful of fresh cilantro, chopped, plus extra sprigs, torn, to garnish

cooked rice or noodles, to serve

The combination of eggplants, bell peppers, and zucchini in this recipe, inspired by the French dish ratatouille, works equally successfully in this delicious curry.

Heat the oil for deep-frying in a preheated wok or a deep pan or deep-fat fryer to 350–375°F/180–190°C, or until a cube of bread browns in 30 seconds. Add the eggplant cubes, in batches, and cook for 45 seconds–1 minute, or until crisp and brown all over. Remove with a slotted spoon and drain on paper towels.

Heat the remaining 2 tablespoons of oil in a separate preheated wok or large skillet. Add the scallions and garlic and stir-fry over medium–high heat for 1 minute. Add the red bell peppers and zucchini and stir-fry for 2–3 minutes. Add the coconut milk and curry paste and bring gently to a boil, stirring occasionally. Add the eggplants and cilantro, then reduce the heat and simmer for 2–3 minutes.

Serve immediately with rice or noodles, garnished with chopped cilantro.

Sweet-and-sour salad

Yum puk ruam mit

Serves 4

¼ cucumber, peeled, halved, and seeded

⅓ cup fresh bean sprouts

1 large carrot, peeled and cut into thin sticks

1 red bell pepper, seeded and sliced

4–5 Chinese cabbages, shredded

1 mango, seeded, peeled, and sliced

few fresh Thai basil leaves, torn into pieces

Dressing

5 tbsp peanut oil

5 scallions, chopped

2 tbsp rice vinegar

1 tbsp superfine sugar

1 small fresh red chile, seeded and finely chopped

2 tbsp pineapple juice

A colorful and surprising mixture of fruit and vegetables that makes a refreshing light lunch or appetizer on warm, sunny days.

Put all the dressing ingredients in a pan and bring gently to a boil. Reduce the heat and simmer for 3–4 minutes, or until the scallions are softened. Let cool.

Put all the prepared salad ingredients in a large bowl. Pour the dressing over, then add the basil and toss to coat.

Cook's tip

Use a teaspoon to scoop the seeds out of the cucumber. To prepare the mango, cut lengthwise either side of the flat central seed. Discard this central slice. Peel the remaining pieces of fruit and slice.

Red curry with mixed leaves

Gang dang puk

Serves 4

2 tbsp peanut or vegetable oil

2 onions, thinly sliced

1 bunch of fine asparagus spears

1³/₄ cups canned coconut milk

2 tbsp red curry paste

3 fresh kaffir lime leaves

8 oz/225 g baby spinach leaves

2 heads bok choy, chopped

1 small head Chinese cabbage, shredded

handful of fresh cilantro, chopped

cooked rice, to serve

This eye-catching mixture of green shoots and leaves should be cooked quickly to retain the varied textures of the ingredients.

Heat the oil in a preheated wok. Add the onions and asparagus and stir-fry over medium–high heat for 1–2 minutes.

Add the coconut milk, curry paste, and lime leaves and bring gently to a boil, stirring occasionally. Add the spinach, bok choy, and Chinese cabbage and cook, stirring, for 2–3 minutes, or until wilted. Add the cilantro and stir well. Serve immediately with rice.

Cook's tip
For nonvegetarians, sprinkle some shredded or diced cooked chicken or cooked shelled shrimp over the cooked rice to accompany the curry.

Rice and Noodles

We usually think of rice and noodles as accompaniments to main dishes, but they can make an equally satisfying lunch or supper in their own right. In Thai cooking, flavor is incorporated into plain rice by first stir-frying it in oil and then cooking it in stock and/or coconut milk.

Egg noodles and rice noodles offer a contrast in both texture and taste, and they also come in different thicknesses. Where noodles form a main part of the dish, they first need to be cooked in boiling water. To prevent them sticking together after draining, rinse under cold running water, ready to use later, or toss them in peanut or vegetable oil or soy sauce. They are usually added to the other ingredients at the final stage.

Pad Thai

Pad thai

Serves 4

8 oz/225 g thick dried rice noodles

2 tbsp peanut or vegetable oil

4 scallions, coarsely chopped

2 garlic cloves, crushed

2 fresh red chiles, seeded
and sliced

8 oz/225 g pork tenderloin,
trimmed and thinly sliced

4 oz/115 g cooked shelled
large shrimp

juice of 1 lime

2 tbsp Thai fish sauce

2 eggs, beaten

1/3 cup fresh bean sprouts

handful of fresh cilantro, chopped

1/3 cup unsalted peanuts, chopped

This traditional Thai dish has many variations, but should always include noodles and peanuts. It is important to use thick rice noodles, which are now widely available.

Soak the noodles in a large pan of boiling water, covered, for 10 minutes until just tender, or according to the package directions. Drain, then rinse under cold running water and set aside.

Heat the oil in a preheated wok. Add the scallions, garlic, and chiles and stir-fry over medium–high heat for 1–2 minutes. Add the pork and stir-fry over high heat for 1–2 minutes, or until browned all over.

Add the shrimp, lime juice, fish sauce, and eggs and stir-fry over medium heat for 2–3 minutes, or until the eggs have set and the shrimp are heated through.

Add the bean sprouts, most of the cilantro, the peanuts, and the noodles and stir-fry for 30 seconds, or until heated through. Serve immediately, garnished with the remaining cilantro.

Egg-fried rice with shrimp and bell peppers

Cow phat gung sai kai

Pink shrimp and red bell peppers cooked with creamed coconut add an exciting, colorful dimension to this well-loved rice dish.

Serves 4

Egg-fried rice

generous 1 cup jasmine rice

1 tbsp peanut or vegetable oil

2 scallions, finely chopped

2 eggs, beaten

handful of fresh cilantro, chopped, plus extra sprigs to garnish

Shrimp and bell peppers

4 tbsp peanut or vegetable oil

2 fresh red chiles, coarsely chopped

6 scallions, coarsely chopped

12 oz/350 g cooked shelled shrimp

2 oz/55 g creamed coconut, chopped and dissolved in ²/₃ cup boiling water

juice of ¹/₂ lemon

6 fresh Thai basil leaves, torn

1 tbsp Thai fish sauce

1 red bell pepper, seeded and cut into strips

Cook the rice in a large pan of lightly salted boiling water for 12–15 minutes until just tender, or according to the package directions. Rinse under cold running water, then fluff up with a fork and let cool completely.

Heat the oil in a preheated wok, then add the scallions and stir-fry over medium–high heat for 30 seconds. Add the rice and stir-fry for 1–2 minutes, or until heated through. Push all the rice to one side of the wok and tilt the pan to let any oil run to the opposite side. While still tilted, add the eggs and cook over medium heat, stirring constantly, for 2–3 minutes, or until set. Return the wok to a level position, then add the cilantro and stir the rice through the cooked eggs. Remove from the heat but keep the rice warm in the wok.

For the shrimp and bell peppers, heat half the oil in a separate preheated wok or large skillet. Add the chiles and scallions and stir-fry over medium–high heat for 1–2 minutes, or until just tender. Add the shrimp, coconut mixture, lemon juice, basil, and fish sauce and bring gently to a boil, stirring occasionally, to ensure that the shrimp are heated through.

Heat the remaining oil in a small skillet, then add the red bell pepper and stir-fry over high heat for 1–2 minutes, or until sizzling and lightly browned. Stir into the shrimp mixture and serve immediately with the egg-fried rice and garnished with sprigs of cilantro.

Cook's tip

Base-line 4 ramekin dishes with parchment paper and divide the rice between them. Press down and then turn out the rice to serve as timbales.

Red roasted pork with peppered noodles

Chad guay taiw moo dang

Serves 2

1 tbsp red curry paste

2 tbsp soy sauce

12 oz/350 g piece pork tenderloin, trimmed

8 oz/225 g fine dried egg noodles

2 tbsp peanut or vegetable oil

1 red onion, chopped

1-inch/2.5-cm piece fresh gingerroot, peeled and finely chopped

1 garlic clove, finely chopped

1 orange bell pepper, seeded and chopped

1 red bell pepper, seeded and chopped

1 tbsp black pepper

1 small bunch of fresh chives, snipped

handful of fresh cilantro, chopped

Red curry paste provides a hot and spicy coating for tender pork tenderloin, which is then sliced and served on top of an egg noodle stir-fry enlivened with both sweet bell peppers and hot black pepper.

Mix the curry paste and soy sauce together in a small bowl and spread over the pork tenderloin. Cover and let marinate in the refrigerator for 1 hour.

Preheat the oven to 400°F/200°C. Roast the pork in the preheated oven for 20–25 minutes, or until cooked through. Remove from the oven, then cover with foil and let rest for 15 minutes.

Meanwhile, cook the noodles in a large pan of boiling water for 4 minutes until just tender, or according to the package directions. Drain, then rinse under cold running water and set aside.

Heat the oil in a preheated wok. Add the onion, ginger, and garlic and stir-fry over medium–high heat for 1–2 minutes. Add the orange and red bell peppers and pepper and stir-fry for 2–3 minutes, or until tender. Stir in the chives and most of the cilantro.

Add the drained noodles to the bell pepper mixture and toss together until well mixed. Divide between 2 serving dishes. Slice the pork and arrange on top of the noodles. Sprinkle with the remaining cilantro and serve immediately.

Thai fish cakes with coconut rice

Tod man pla gap cow krati

Serves 4

Fish cakes

1 lb/450 g skinned white fish fillets, such as cod or coley, coarsely cut into chunks

6 scallions, finely chopped

1–2 tbsp red curry paste

1 tbsp Thai fish sauce

2 egg whites

peanut or vegetable oil, for pan-frying

Coconut rice

2 tbsp peanut or vegetable oil

1 onion, chopped

generous 1 cup jasmine rice

1¾ cups canned coconut milk

1 tbsp red curry paste

1 tbsp Thai fish sauce

handful of fresh cilantro, chopped

To serve

lime wedges

sweet chili dipping sauce (optional)

It's quick and easy to make the fish cake mixture, but you need time to pat it into shapes and cook them. You can serve them on their own with a sweet chili dipping sauce as an appetizer.

For the fish cakes, put all the ingredients except the oil in a food processor and process to a coarse paste. Use damp hands to shape into 12 small, flat cakes. Cover and chill in the refrigerator for 30 minutes.

For the coconut rice, heat the oil in a preheated wok, then add the onion and stir-fry over medium–high heat for 2 minutes. Add the rice and stir-fry for 30 seconds, or until coated with the oil. Add the coconut milk, curry paste, and fish sauce and bring gently to a boil, stirring occasionally. Reduce the heat and simmer gently for 10–15 minutes, or until the rice is tender, adding a little boiling water or stock if necessary. Stir in the cilantro.

Meanwhile, heat enough oil for pan-frying to cover the bottom of a large skillet. Add the fish cakes, in batches, and cook over medium heat for 3 minutes, then turn over and cook on the other side for 2 minutes, or until browned on both sides. Remove with a slotted spoon and drain on paper towels. Keep the cooked fish cakes warm while you cook the remainder.

Spoon the rice onto serving plates. Top with a few fish cakes and serve with lime wedges and the sweet chili dipping sauce, if using.

Chile rice with stir-fried beef

Cow phad nue prik

Thickly sliced beef tenderloin can take a strong flavor and makes a great combination when served with hot chile rice. A good red wine would be ideal served with this meal.

Serves 4

Chile rice

2 tbsp peanut or vegetable oil

5 scallions, chopped

2 oz/55 g fine green beans, trimmed and halved

2 fresh red chiles, seeded and sliced

1 1/8 cups basmati rice

2 1/2 cups beef stock

Stir-fried beef

2 tbsp peanut or vegetable oil

1 onion, cut into wedges

1 green bell pepper, seeded and cut into chunks

1-inch/2.5-cm piece fresh gingerroot, peeled and finely chopped

12 oz/350 g beef tenderloin, cut into strips

6 tbsp oyster sauce

2 tbsp soy sauce

1 tsp jaggery

handful of fresh cilantro, chopped

To make the chile rice, heat the oil in a preheated wok. Add the scallions, green beans, and chiles and stir-fry over medium–high heat for 1–2 minutes. Add the rice and stir-fry for 2–3 minutes. Add the stock and bring to a boil, stirring occasionally. Reduce the heat and simmer gently for 10–15 minutes, or until the rice is tender, adding more stock if necessary. Remove from the heat but keep the rice warm in the wok.

To make the stir-fried beef, heat the oil in a separate preheated wok or large skillet. Add the onion, green bell pepper, and ginger and stir-fry over medium–high heat for 30 seconds. Add the beef and stir-fry over high heat for 1–2 minutes, or until browned all over. Add the oyster sauce, soy sauce, and sugar and stir-fry for 2–3 minutes, or until heated through. Serve immediately with the chile rice, sprinkled with the cilantro.

Cook's tip

To give the stir-fry extra crunch and color, halve baby corn and add to the wok or skillet with the onion, green bell pepper, and gingerroot.

Squid and shrimp laksa

Tom ka talay

Most fish suppliers and supermarkets sell squid ready cleaned so that you don't have to prepare it yourself. It usually comes frozen, so you will need to thaw it in the refrigerator before using.

Serves 4

8 oz/225 g dried rice noodles

3 cups canned coconut milk

2 fish stock cubes

3 fresh kaffir lime leaves

2 tbsp red curry paste

1 bunch of scallions, coarsely chopped

2 fresh red chiles, seeded and coarsely chopped

8 oz/225 g raw squid, cleaned and cut into rings

8 oz/225 g large raw shrimp, shelled and deveined

handful of fresh cilantro, chopped, plus leaves to garnish

Soak the noodles in a pan of boiling water for 4 minutes, covered, until just tender, or according to the package directions. Drain, then rinse under cold running water and set aside.

Put the coconut milk, stock cubes, lime leaves, curry paste, scallions, and chiles in a large pan and bring gently to a boil, stirring occasionally. Reduce the heat and simmer, stirring occasionally, for 2–3 minutes, or until the stock cubes and paste have dissolved. Add the squid and shrimp and simmer for 1–2 minutes, or until the squid has plumped up and the shrimp have turned pink. Add the cooked noodles and cilantro and stir well. Serve in soup bowls, garnished with cilantro leaves.

Cook's tip

Fresh kaffir lime leaves can be kept in a freezer bag in the freezer. Take out as many as you need at the time. Dried lime leaves are also available in packages, but the fresh ones add much more flavor.

Chicken curry with fried noodles

Gang gai mee grob

Serves 4

2 tbsp peanut or vegetable oil, plus extra for deep-frying

4 skinless, boneless chicken breasts, about 4 oz/115 g each, cut into 1-inch/2.5-cm cubes

2 red onions, coarsely chopped

5 scallions, coarsely chopped

2 garlic cloves, finely chopped

1 fresh green chile, seeded and finely chopped

6 oz/175 g shiitake mushrooms, thickly sliced

2 tbsp green curry paste

1³/₄ cups canned coconut milk

1¹/₄ cups chicken stock

2 fresh kaffir lime leaves

handful of fresh cilantro, chopped

handful of fresh chives, snipped

1 oz/25 g stir-fry rice noodles

cooked rice, to serve (optional)

The rice noodles puff up really quickly in hot oil—great entertainment for children to watch at a safe distance—but take care, as they are done in a matter of seconds.

Heat the oil in a preheated wok. Add the chicken cubes, in batches, and stir-fry over medium–high heat for 3–4 minutes, or until lightly browned all over. Remove with a slotted spoon, then transfer to a plate and set aside.

Add the red onions and scallions, garlic, and chile to the wok and stir-fry over medium heat, adding a little more oil if necessary, for 2–3 minutes, or until softened but not browned. Add the mushrooms and stir-fry over high heat for 30 seconds. Return the chicken to the wok.

Add the curry paste, coconut milk, stock, and lime leaves and bring gently to a boil, stirring occasionally. Reduce the heat and simmer gently for 4–5 minutes, or until the chicken is tender and cooked through. Stir in the cilantro and chives.

Meanwhile, heat the oil for deep-frying in a separate wok or deep-sided skillet to 350–375°F/180–190°C, or until a cube of bread browns in 30 seconds. Divide the noodles into 4 portions and cook, one portion at a time, for about 2 seconds until puffed up and crisp. Remove with a slotted spoon and drain on paper towels.

Serve the curry with rice, if using, and topped with the crispy noodles.

Spicy chicken kabobs
with cilantro rice

Gai kebab gao cow

Serves 4

Chicken kabobs

3 tbsp oyster sauce

2 tbsp soy sauce, plus extra
for serving

1-inch/2.5-cm piece fresh
gingerroot, peeled and finely
chopped

4 tbsp honey

2 tsp dark brown sugar

2 tsp cornstarch

4 skinless, boneless chicken
breasts, about 4 oz/115 g each,
cut into 1-inch/2.5-cm cubes

2 red bell peppers, seeded and cut
into 1-inch/2.5-cm squares

Cilantro rice

2 tbsp peanut or vegetable oil

6 scallions, chopped

generous 1 cup jasmine rice

2¹/₂ cups chicken stock

4 oz/115 g bok choy,
coarsely chopped

4 oz/115 g baby spinach leaves

large handful of fresh cilantro,
chopped

The honey adds sweetness and stickiness to the chicken. Cook over high heat to char the chicken before finishing off in the oven.

Soak 8 bamboo skewers in cold water for at least 30 minutes. For the kabobs, mix all the ingredients except the chicken cubes and red bell peppers together in a bowl. Add the chicken cubes and toss to coat. Cover and let marinate in the refrigerator for 2 hours.

Preheat the oven to 375°F/190°C. Divide the chicken cubes and red bell pepper squares between the skewers, threading alternately onto the skewers. Heat a ridged grill pan until hot, then add the skewers and cook over high heat for 3–4 minutes, turning occasionally, until browned all over. Transfer to a cookie sheet and cook in the preheated oven for an additional 10–12 minutes, or until cooked through.

Meanwhile, to make the cilantro rice, heat the oil in a preheated wok. Add the scallions and stir-fry over medium–high heat for 30 seconds, or until softened. Add the rice and stir-fry for 2–3 minutes. Add the stock and bring to a boil, stirring occasionally. Reduce the heat and simmer for 10–12 minutes, or until the rice is tender, adding more stock or boiling water if necessary. Add the bok choy, spinach, and cilantro and cook, stirring, for 1–2 minutes, or until wilted.

Spoon the rice onto serving plates and top with the chicken kabobs and a little extra soy sauce, then serve immediately.

Spring vegetable rice

Khao pat puk

Serves 4

2 tbsp peanut or vegetable oil

2 shallots, chopped

2 garlic cloves, crushed

1¹⁄₈ cups basmati rice

2¹⁄₂ cups chicken stock

1 tbsp red curry paste

1 tsp Thai fish sauce

3 tbsp soy sauce

6 oz/175 g baby corn, halved lengthwise

4 oz/115 g baby carrots, halved lengthwise

2 oz/55 g sugar snap peas

¹⁄₃ cup fresh bean sprouts

4 tbsp sesame seeds

handful of fresh cilantro, chopped

2 tbsp sesame oil

An ideal quick and easy supper after the long winter, when all the baby spring vegetables come onto the supermarket shelves. You can also add asparagus spears to the medley when available.

Heat the oil in a preheated wok. Add the shallots and garlic and stir-fry over medium–high heat for 1–2 minutes. Add the rice and stir-fry for 2–3 minutes. Add the stock, curry paste, fish sauce, and soy sauce and bring to a boil, stirring occasionally. Reduce the heat and simmer for 10–12 minutes, or until the rice is tender, adding more stock or boiling water, if necessary.

Meanwhile, cook the baby corn and carrots in a pan of lightly salted boiling water for 2–3 minutes, or until just tender. Add the sugar snap peas and cook for 1 minute. Add the bean sprouts and stir well, then drain.

Heat a dry skillet until hot, then add the sesame seeds and cook over medium–high heat, shaking the skillet frequently, for 30–45 seconds, or until lightly browned.

Add the drained vegetables, cilantro, and sesame oil to the rice and serve immediately, sprinkled with the toasted sesame seeds.

Index